In the text, numbers in parentheses refer to the pages on which artifacts appear.

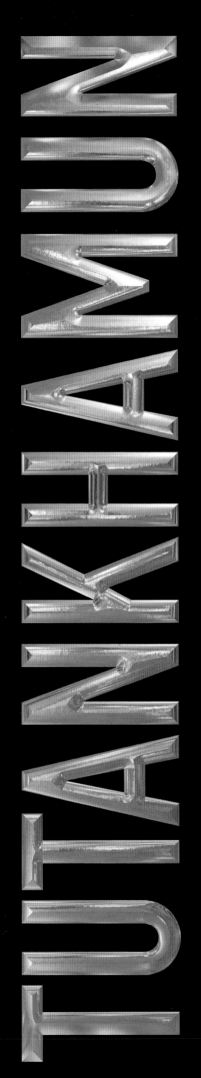

TUTANKHAMUN

TREASURES OF THE GOLDEN PHARAOH

A GIFT FROM THE BOY KING

ZAHI HAWASS

MELCHER MEDIA

IMG

The Egyptian Ministry of Antiquities has launched this exhibit, *Tutankhamun: Treasures of the Golden Pharaoh*, to celebrate the most important archaeological discovery of the century: the intact tomb of Tutankhamun, known to Egyptologists as KV62.

The exhibit will take visitors back to the five years that Howard Carter spent searching for the tomb, a quest that led to so many important and emotional moments: the discovery of the steps to the tomb, Carter's look through a hole to see the treasures and his famous words, "Wonderful things," the opening of the sarcophagus and the removal of the gilded coffins, the sight of the mummy encased in the golden mask, the recovery of 150 beautiful amulets and objects from the mummy wrappings, and the revelation of the king's face.

The exhibit commemorates the centennial of Tutankhamun's discovery and is accompanied by the construction of the Grand Egyptian Museum (GEM). In this museum, the most important cultural project in the world, we will be able to display all the objects of Tutankhamun in a beautiful exhibit. This souvenir book will be a memento by which everyone can remember the anniversary of this great discovery.

I myself will never forget the magical moment in 2005 when I lifted the lid of the sarcophagus and the third coffin in which the mummy lay and met face to face with the king I fondly call "the Golden Boy." This exhibit will bring the magic, mystery, and thrill of ancient Egypt to all who visit. None of us will ever forget the stories of the pharaoh's curse and the magic it brought to the discovery a hundred years ago. Every artifact in this exhibit is displayed in a way that will capture your heart and make all of us dream of the land of the pharaohs.

Zahi Hawass

CHRONOLOGY OF ANCIENT EGYPTIAN HISTORY

PREDYNASTIC PERIOD ca. 4400–3100 BC

EARLY DYNASTIC PERIOD
(First–Second Dynasties)
ca. 3100–2649 BC

FIRST DYNASTY ca. 3100–2910 BC

SECOND DYNASTY ca. 2910–2649 BC

OLD KINGDOM
(Third–Eighth Dynasties)   **ca. 2649–2100 BC**

THIRD DYNASTY   ca. 2469–2575 BC

FOURTH DYNASTY   ca. 2575–2465 BC

FIFTH DYNASTY   ca. 2465–2353 BC

SIXTH DYNASTY   ca. 2353–2152 BC

SEVENTH–EIGHTH DYNASTIES   ca. 2151–2100 BC

MIDDLE KINGDOM
(Late Eleventh–Early Thirteenth Dynasties)   **ca. 2030–1640 BC**

LATE ELEVENTH DYNASTY
(Post-Unification)   ca. 2030–1981 BC

TWELFTH DYNASTY   ca. 1981–1802 BC

EARLY THIRTEENTH DYNASTY   ca. 1802–1640 BC

FIRST INTERMEDIATE PERIOD
(Ninth–Early Eleventh Dynasties)   **ca. 2100–2030 BC**

NINTH–TENTH DYNASTIES   ca. 2100–2030 BC

EARLY ELEVENTH DYNASTY
(Pre-Unification)   ca. 2151–2030 BC

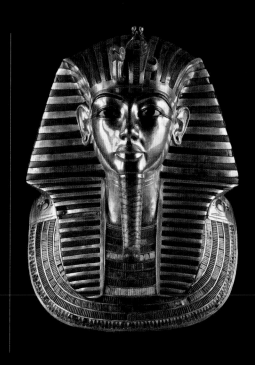

NEW KINGDOM
(Eighteenth–Twentieth Dynasties)

ca. 1550 – 1070 BC

EIGHTEENTH DYNASTY

ca. 1550 –1295 BC

NINETEENTH DYNASTY
(Ramesside)

ca. 1295 –1186 BC

TWENTIETH DYNASTY
(Ramesside)

ca. 1186 –1070 BC

SECOND INTERMEDIATE PERIOD
(Late Thirteenth – Seventeenth Dynasties)

ca. 1640–1550 BC

LATE THIRTEENTH DYNASTY

ca. 1640-1575 BC

FOURTEENTH DYNASTY

ca. 1700 BC

FIFTEENTH DYNASTY
(Hyksos)

ca. 1650–1540 BC

SIXTEENTH DYNASTY

ca. 1650 BC

SEVENTEENTH DYNASTY
(Theban)

ca. 1570–1550 BC

THIRD INTERMEDIATE PERIOD
(Twenty-First – Twenty-Fifth Dynasties)

ca. 1070–664 BC

TWENTY-FIRST DYNASTY

ca. 1070–945 BC

TWENTY-SECOND DYNASTY

ca. 945–712 BC

TWENTY-THIRD DYNASTY

ca. 818–700 BC

TWENTY-FOURTH DYNASTY

ca. 724–712 BC

TWENTY-FIFTH DYNASTY
(Kushite)

ca. 733–664 BC

LATE PERIOD
(Twenty-Sixth–Thirtieth Dynasties)   **664–332 BC**

TWENTY-SIXTH DYNASTY
(Saite)   **664–525 BC**

TWENTY-SEVENTH DYNASTY
(First Persian Period)   **525–404 BC**

TWENTY-EIGHTH DYNASTY   ca. 460 BC

TWENTY-NINTH DYNASTY   339–390 BC

THIRTIETH DYNASTY   390–343 BC

SECOND PERSIAN PERIOD   343–332 BC

ROMAN PERIOD   **30 BC–AD 364**

PTOLEMAIC PERIOD   **303–30 BC**

MACEDONIAN PERIOD   **332–305 BC**

Before Egypt was ruled by pharaohs, during a time called the Predynastic Period, cultures rose and flourished throughout the Nile River Valley, which offered rich land and waters for hunting, herding, and agriculture. In Upper Egypt (the south), stratified societies developed at several sites, which evolved into powerful chiefdoms. Through a long process, these chiefdoms in turn became a single kingdom. The culture of this Upper Egyptian kingdom spread slowly northward to Lower Egypt (the north). Eventually, one king ruled the entire Nile Valley, from the first cataract at Aswan all the way to the coast of the Mediterranean Sea. The first pharaoh had emerged.

The Egyptians conceived of their gradual period of state formation as the conquest of one kingdom over another, even though no single Lower Egyptian kingdom ever existed. The concept of duality was an important one in pharaonic times, so the idea of an Upper and Lower Egypt was appealing. They devised many ways to express this concept, which they called *sema-tawy*, ("union of the Two Lands") The king often appears under the protection of the cobra, representing the patron goddess of Lower Egypt, Wadjet, and the vulture, Nekhbet, who was the patron goddess of Upper Egypt (p. 41). Each of the Two Lands had its own crown—the white crown for the south (p. 61) and the red crown for the north (p. 52)—which the king might wear separately or as the combined double crown (p. 37). The lotus (p. 60) and papyrus were the floral symbols for Upper and Lower Egypt. All of these reminded the people of the divided Egypt of the very distant past, now united and whole under the rule of the one true king of Egypt.

The Third Dynasty marked the beginning of the Old Kingdom, a new era of Egyptian history when, for the first time, Egyptian kings were powerful and wealthy enough to undertake royal construction programs that were enormous even by today's standards. The administrative capital of the country was Memphis, which is now in the area of Mit Rahina, in the vicinity of modern Cairo. Kings sent expeditions to Sinai, the Western Desert, and deep into Nubia to engage in trade with neighboring cultures, to mine gold, and to quarry stone. The growing economy gave Egypt the necessary resources for huge construction projects, most famously the Great Pyramid, constructed by King Khufu at Giza to serve as his house of eternity. Many other pyramids were built, as were temples for the gods. Since the earliest times, kings had identified themselves with the god Horus, and during the Old Kingdom, they began to call themselves "sons of Re," the sun god.

Through the course of the Old Kingdom, the Third through the Sixth Dynasties, royal power slowly waned, and high officials, from families unrelated to the king's, gained more control over matters in Egypt. This political change, and possibly a change in climate, brought Egypt into a so-called dark age, the First Intermediate Period, when the Two Lands had disintegrated and the power of the state lay in the hands of strongmen who ruled chiefdoms scattered along the length of the Nile. These local rulers sometimes allied themselves with and sometimes challenged rulers in the north who styled themselves kings of all Egypt.

MAP OF ANCIENT EGYPT, INCLUDING UPPER EGYPT, LOWER EGYPT, AND KUSH.

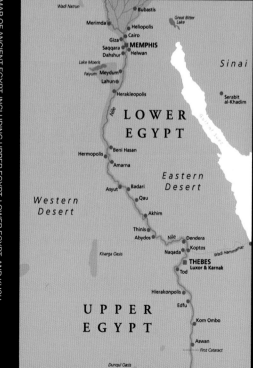

HAPI TYING THE PAPYRUS AND REED PLANTS IN THE *SEMA-TAWY* SYMBOL FOR THE UNIFICATION OF UPPER AND LOWER EGYPT.

THE SUN COURT OF AMENHOTEP III AT LUXOR TEMPLE.

After a hundred years or so of disunity, a very capable, ambitious king rose to power in the Upper Egyptian city of Thebes (modern Luxor). Through force of arms, he consolidated the Two Lands again and brought the people of Egypt together under his sole rule. His name was Mentuhotep II, and his reign marked the beginning of the Middle Kingdom, the second great age in Egyptian history. This was a period of cultural flowering. Literature and jewelry making reached their peaks at this time. Rulers of the Middle Kingdom built a line of fortresses along the river at the second cataract in Nubia and in the north in Sinai, in order to regulate trade with the foreigners in these regions and guard Egypt's borders from its enemies. In the area of modern Fayoum, one of the early Middle Kingdom rulers, Amenemhat I, founded a new capital city, Itjtawy ("Seizer of the Two Lands"). Thebes remained important as a religious center, and one of its gods, Amun ("the Hidden One") became prominent. Mentuhotep II was buried on the Theban west bank, but later kings were buried elsewhere. In the north, other kings built pyramids that never reached the enormous size of those constructed during the Fourth Dynasty. These were also built somewhat more economically, with enormous amounts of mud brick and rubble.

During the Middle Kingdom, people from the Levant began to settle in the northeastern part of the Nile Delta. These people grew in number and influence as they came to hold important positions in the royal court.

The more the power of the king diminished, the more control they gained over administrative matters, until they had at last established their own kingdom with a capital at Avaris, a city along the Pelusiac branch of the Nile. Another influx of Levantines, known as the Hyksos, took over the north of Egypt and founded their own ruling dynasty, the Fifteenth. They ruled the north of Egypt for the next century or so, while a weakened Egyptian dynasty, the Sixteenth, ruled the south.

The Sixteenth and the Seventeenth Egyptian dynasties ruled from Thebes, and once again this southern city gave rise to a ruler who would reunite the Two Lands. The Theban king, Seqenenre Tao, and many more Egyptian soldiers sacrificed their lives in the fight against the Hyksos. Seqenenre Tao was succeeded by Kamose, who continued his struggle. Ahmose, Seqenenre's son and Kamose's successor, took command of the army and pushed forward farther to the north. In battle, both sides used new military equipment that had been introduced from Asia: horse-drawn chariots (pp. 48, 54) and compound bows (p.49), which gave archers greater range than the older type of bow. Ahmose voyaged downriver to the north with his army, sacked Avaris, and drove the Hyksos out of Egypt. Egypt was reunified under a new dynasty at the opening of a new golden age, known today as the New Kingdom.

Ahmose's Eighteenth Dynasty was one of the strongest to ever rule Egypt. His descendants were so militarily powerful that

they expanded the empire until its southern extent was to the area of modern Khartoum in Sudan and the holdings of its vassal states in the north reached the southern border of modern Turkey. The Egyptians remembered what had happened before, at the end of the Middle Kingdom, and determined that Egypt would never again fall prey to outsiders. Booty from war and merchandise from peaceful trade with neighboring empires added to Egypt's wealth and splendor. Ahmose and his successors credited the god Amun with their victories, and the god's temple and priesthood grew wealthy and influential. For their burial place, most rulers of the New Kingdom selected a valley in the hills to the west of Amun's sacred city of Thebes, overlooked by a peak that resembles a pyramid. Today called the Valley of the Kings, this place offered security to the dead kings: here they and the treasures necessary for their afterlife could be hidden away and guarded.

Egypt's wealth was so great that foreign kings claimed that "gold was like dust" there. Such wealth made it possible for King Amenhotep III, Tutankhamun's grandfather, to undertake major building projects all over Egypt and in Nubia. These were so numerous and of such magnitude that some scholars consider him to be the greatest builder the New Kingdom ever saw. Egypt was the most powerful and the wealthiest empire of the ancient world, and the ancient Egyptian civilization was at its zenith.

RECONSTRUCTED WALL DECORATIONS FROM THE TEMPLE OF AKHENATEN AT KARNAK. THE BUILDING WAS LATER DEMOLISHED AND ITS 289 STONE BLOCKS (*TALATATS*) WERE USED TO FORM THE CORE OF THE NINTH PYLON OF THE AMUN TEMPLE DURING HOREMHEB'S REIGN.

AKHENATEN AND HIS FAMILY WORSHIPING THE ATEN, WITH CHARACTERISTIC RAYS SEEN EMANATING FROM THE SOLAR DISK.

THE BUST OF NEFERTITI, THE GREAT ROYAL WIFE OF THE PHARAOH AKHENATEN.

Amenhotep III had been a boy king, coming to the throne at the age of perhaps ten. His wife, Queen Tiye, was a commoner whom he loved greatly, and together they had two sons. Prince Thutmose is generally believed to have been the elder and Amenhotep III's intended successor. However, Thutmose died before his father, which meant that the throne would go to his younger brother, Amenhotep. Some scholars believe that, in his later years, Amenhotep III had Amenhotep IV rule alongside him. Others believe there was no coregency and that Amenhotep IV assumed the throne only after Amenhotep III's death. In any case, whether his father sat on the throne with him or not, the beginning of Amenhotep IV's reign marked a new turning point that would affect the art and culture of Egypt long after his death.

Unlike most of his predecessors, this king was not fond of military conquests. His father had gone into battle only a couple of times as a young man, so Egypt saw no war during Amenhotep IV's lifetime. But Amenhotep IV would bring a very different kind of battle to Egypt. After the fifth year of his reign, Amenhotep IV revolutionized ancient Egyptian religion—he decided there was one, and only one, god: the Aten, which was the solar disk, the most abstract form in which the Egyptians represented their sun god, Re. He eliminated the worship of Amun, the "king of the gods," by shutting down all of Amun's temples and ordering the obliteration of Amun's name everywhere it could be found.

As king of Egypt, and as the son of the Aten, Amenhotep IV was the god's representative on earth. The Aten spoke directly and only to him. The god's blessing flowed through him and other members of the royal family. Amenhotep IV changed his name from "Amun is satisfied," to "Akhenaten," which means "he who is effective for Aten." And, because Thebes was so closely associated with the god whom Akhenaten so despised, he abandoned the city. The Aten required temples on virgin land, where no other god had ever been worshipped. About 400 kilometers (250 miles) downriver from Thebes, Akhenaten found such a site. In this part of the country, the steep hills of the Eastern Desert come quite close to the river, but here was a place where they surrounded a sort of large desert "bay," giving more than enough room for a city of temples, palaces, and houses for courtiers and for the thousands of lower-class Egyptians necessary for a royal city to function. The city he founded here was named Akhetaten, "Horizon of the Aten." Today, the site is called Tell el-Amarna.

Before becoming king, Akhenaten had married a woman named Nefertiti, who, like his mother, was a commoner. By the time of the great move from Thebes, they had three daughters, Meritaten, Meketaten, and Ankhesenpaaten. Nefertiti was a strong, politically astute woman who would come to rule alongside her husband. She appeared beside him in the temples and in public appearances, along with their growing number of children, all girls. Nefertiti would give birth to six surviving daughters, but no sons.

Despite Nefertiti's strong character, Akhenaten elevated a secondary wife, named Kiya, to prominence. Some speculate that this unknown wife was a foreign princess for whom Amenhotep III had negotiated a bride price but who had arrived only after the old king's death. Some scholars believe that Kiya was the mother of Akhenaten's son, a boy named Tutankhaten ("the living image of the Aten"), and her disappearance from history at the same time as Tutankhaten's birth might suggest that she died in childbirth. But all of this is speculation. DNA tests on royal mummies from this period revealed that Tutankhamun's mother was a daughter of Amenhotep III and Tiye and, therefore, Akhenaten's sister. Tutankhaten was probably born at one of the palaces of Tell el-Amarna.

Late in his reign, Akhenaten took a coregent. This second ruler, who used the name Ankhkheperure or its feminine form, Ankhetkheperure, was most likely Nefertiti (pp. 14, 23, 29). She outlived him, though only briefly. Tutankhamun may have been old enough to remember the death of his father in the seventeenth year of his reign. The cause of Akhenaten's death remains a mystery. His religious revolution did not survive him. Even during the reign of Ankhkheperure, the worship of Amun was being restored.

Ankhkheperure had an independent reign of only a year or less. She was succeeded by her stepson, the eight- or nine-year-old Tutankhaten. Despite coming to the throne so young, he would rule Egypt for only about ten years before his own untimely death.

TUTANKHAMUN: FROM AMARNA TO THEBES

3.

A DETAIL FROM THE INLAID BACK PANEL OF THE GOLDEN THRONE (CARTER 91), DEPICTING TUTANKHAMUN WITH HIS WIFE ANKHESENAMUN ATTENDING HIM.

Although the identity of Tutankhaten's mother remains a mystery, his nurse is known. This was a woman named Maia, who was given an elaborate tomb at Saqqara, an unusual honor for a woman. One of its scenes portrays her intimate relationship with the young king. She sits on a chair and holds on her lap Tutankhaten—shown as a small boy wearing the blue crown.

Tutankhaten spent his early childhood in the palaces of Amarna along with Akhenaten's six daughters, his half-sisters. There is an inscription from Amarna that appears to name both Tutankhaten and the princess Ankhesenpaaten, Akhenaten and Nefertiti's third daughter.

Life in the palaces at Amarna came to an end soon after the deaths of Akhenaten and Nefertiti. For his coronation ceremony, Tutankhaten was brought to Thebes, the city of Amun that his father had permanently abandoned. Through a series of rituals performed in the temple of Amun at Karnak, the young prince was transformed into the king of Egypt, the living Horus, representative of the gods on earth. The choice of Karnak temple for this event left no doubt that the Aten had been demoted back to its place as another of Re's

many aspects, and that Amun had resumed his proper place as king of the gods and the chief god of the Egyptian state.

Thebes once again became Egypt's glorious religious capital, which the king would visit for important religious festivals. A royal decree issued in the name of the young king described the restorations undertaken at temples in Thebes, Memphis, and elsewhere. Memphis, Egypt's ancient administrative center in the north of the country, had always been important, even during Akhenaten's reign, and it was here that the new court based itself. Here, rather than in Thebes, was the king's usual residence.

The forces behind all of these decisions were the adults in the royal court, as Tutankhaten was too young. Another decision certainly in the hands of Tutankhaten's elders was a change of name. Mention of the Aten was no longer suitable. So both king and queen were given new names that rejected the "Atenism" of their father and commemorated the restoration of Amun as the chief god of the state: Tutankhamun and Ankhesenamun.

Egypt's busy religious calendar kept the royal court on the move throughout the country, but while at Memphis, Tutankhamun

THREE SCENES DECORATING THE NORTH WALL OF THE BURIAL CHAMBER IN THE TOMB OF TUTANKHAMUN (KV62). LEFT TO RIGHT: OSIRIS WELCOMING TUTANKHAMUN TO THE UNDERWORLD, FOLLOWED BY HIS *KA*; THE GODDESS NUT GREETING TUTANKHAMUN TO THE REALM OF THE GODS; AND TUTANKHAMUN APPEARING AS OSIRIS, LORD OF THE UNDERWORLD, BEFORE AY, HIS SUCCESSOR, WHO PERFORMS THE "OPENING OF THE MOUTH" CEREMONY ON THE RIGHT.

and Ankhesenamun could enjoy boating together in the marshes of the Nile Delta (p. 3) and playing board games in the palace gardens. In the desert around Memphis, Tutankhamun practiced what became his favorite sports, chariot driving and hunting (p. 48, 54). He did not allow his deformed feet and need for walking sticks to interfere with his pleasures. He had been trained since childhood to shoot a bow and arrow (p. 49), as were all kings and princes of Egypt.

This was not merely for sport. The foremost responsibility of an Egyptian king was to maintain *maat*, a word that encompassed the Egyptian concept of truth, cosmic and social order, and justice. He was high priest of all the gods, personally responsible for appeasing them through temple ritual. By hunting wild animals, he demonstrated his mastery over the natural world and the forces of chaos that threatened the Egyptian way of life (pp. 48, 54). He also had to maintain the security of the country's borders and subdue Egypt's human enemies (p. 37).

Being so young, in governing the Egyptian state Tutankhamun needed the assistance of experienced courtiers, many of whom had served his father and even his

grandfather. One of his closest advisers was Ay, his vizier, who might have been the brother of Amenhotep III's wife, Tiye, although this remains uncertain. The overseer of the treasury and royal building projects was a man named Maya. Because Tutankhamun had no children, another courtier was appointed to serve as crown prince. This was Horemheb, the general who commanded the Egyptian army. Late in Tutankhamun's short reign, Horemheb led campaigns in western Asia against Egypt's northern enemies, the Hittites.

Horemheb seems to have been away when Tutankhamun unexpectedly died, probably due to an injury sustained while driving his chariot. That may be why the crown prince did not succeed the young king. This honor fell to Ay.

Maya, the treasurer, was the one who oversaw preparations for the burial, which would take place in the Valley of the Kings. After courtiers ceremonially conveyed Tutankhamun's mummy from the embalmers' workshop to the tomb and stood the mummy before the entrance, Ay performed the ceremony of the Opening of the Mouth, a complex ritual traditionally enacted by a son for his dead father. This allowed the dead

the netherworld. This also established Ay as Tutankhamun's rightful heir and, consequently, as rightful king of Egypt.

The widowed Ankhesenamun remained queen beside the new king, but likely not for long. The only evidence of their union is a ring with her name and Ay's. At this point she vanished from history. Ay's spouse of many years, a woman named Tiye, served as his great royal wife during his four-year reign.

Upon Ay's death, Horemheb assumed the throne that had been promised him if Tutankhamun produced no children. Although he served Tutankhamun faithfully insofar as we know, and he may have married Nefertiti's sister Mutnodjmet, he ordered the names of Tutankhamun, Ankhesenamun, Ay, and Akhenaten hacked out of all the monuments. In many cases, he replaced Tutankhamun's and Ay's names with his own. He also ordered that the city of Amarna be dismantled.

Tutankhamun's name was forgotten. It would have remained lost to one of history's many black holes if it had not been for one man with a dream, an Englishman by the name of Howard Carter.

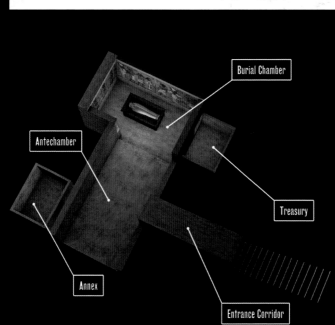

Burial Chamber

Antechamber

Treasury

Annex

Entrance Corridor

Howard Carter first came to Egypt in 1891 as an artist to copy the colorful scenes in the Middle Kingdom tombs of Beni Hassan, in the modern governorate of Minya. At this time, the "father of modern Egyptology," Sir William Flinders Petrie, was working at Amarna, which is also in Minya. Here, with Petrie's guidance, Carter learned to excavate, which laid the foundation for his career as a great archaeologist.

In 1899, the Antiquities Service appointed him to be chief inspector of Upper Egypt, which included Thebes and the Valley of the Kings. This was a time when Egypt allowed foreign excavators to bring a portion of their discoveries home with them, which lured wealthy benefactors to fund excavations in search of beautiful or interesting artifacts for their private collections. Because the tombs of some New Kingdom pharaohs were yet to be found, Carter had hopes of making significant discoveries in the Valley of the Kings, including the tomb of the Eighteenth Dynasty king Thutmose IV. In 1899, he had met a wealthy American businessman, Theodore Davis, who was visiting Luxor. Davis had demonstrated his willingness to fund an excavation, so Carter persuaded him to sponsor excavations in the valley.

This led to a streak of discoveries in the valley with Carter and, later, other Egyptologists. The first season, in 1902, provided enough to whet Davis's appetite for more—Carter had found a piece of a stone vase with the name of Thutmose IV on it, which led him to suspect that the king's tomb would be nearby. During the next season, in 1903, Carter found a place where the bedrock had been cut. Excavation revealed a buried stairway leading down to the entrance of an obviously plundered tomb, and in the rubble he found another object naming this same king. That the newly discovered tomb, called KV43, belonged to Thutmose IV was made certain by a discovery in front of the uppermost step: foundation deposits with ritual and votive objects inscribed with the name of Thutmose IV. Carter had found his first royal tomb in the Valley of the Kings. Although thoroughly looted in antiquity, it still contained much of great interest: the decorated walls, the sarcophagus, parts of a chariot, objects of glass and faience, figures of the king carved in wood and coated in bitumen, and much else.

Their next task was physically more challenging: relocating KV20, a tomb packed with debris washed into it by the flash floods that sometimes strike the region. Its outer chamber had first been explored in the late eighteenth century, but, daunted by the dense, flood-packed dirt and rock that plugged the rest, no one had excavated further. In 1903, Carter and Davis's team undertook this task. Because they recovered objects inscribed for Hatshepsut, the controversial female pharaoh who ruled Egypt during the early Eighteenth Dynasty, they concluded that KV20 had been her tomb. But in the 1970s, British Egyptologist John Romer proved that this tomb had been created for her father, Thutmose I, who was probably the first king to be buried in the Valley of the Kings.

The Antiquities Service diverted Carter's career by pulling him from Luxor to serve as chief inspector of Lower Egypt, the northern part of the country, in 1904. Davis remained in the south to continue his exploration in the valley with another British Egyptologist, James Quibell. On Davis's behalf, Quibell found another non-royal tomb, KV46. The entrance to the tomb retained its plaster blocking, stamped with the official seal of the royal cemetery, which depicted the jackal god Anubis above nine captive enemies. However, a small hole that penetrated through both the outer and inner doorways suggested that robbers had reached the tomb and probably stolen jewelry and other small objects of value. Quibell and his team were right, but what remained in KV46 were spectacular examples of funerary furniture, along with the mummies of the owners. These were Yuya and Tjuya, parents of Queen Tiye, Amenhotep III's great royal wife, and, as we now know, the great-grandparents of Tutankhamun. Despite the good work they did as a team on this discovery, Quibell and Davis quarreled and ended their working relationship.

This did not end Davis's appetite for further work in the Valley of the Kings. His next collaborator was Edward Ayrton. Together they found several more private tombs, as well as the royal tomb of the Eighteenth Dynasty's last king, Horemheb (KV57), and the tomb of Siptah (KV47), a ruler of the late Nineteenth Dynasty. Most important among their discoveries was the curious KV55. Here they found objects from the Amarna Period, including a large gilded wooden shrine from the burial of Queen Tiye and, in a golden coffin, the remains of a mummy that, a century later, would prove to be Tutankhamun's father, Akhenaten.

Ayrton is credited with being the first to find objects inscribed with Tutankhamun's birth name (Tutankhaten) (p. 27) and throne name (Nebkheperure) in the Valley of the Kings. First, while working around KV48 (a non-royal tomb) during the 1905–1906 season, he found a faience cup. In 1907, he discovered a large pit, KV54, that contained a variety of objects, including several pottery jars, a miniature gilded mummy mask, and a piece of linen on which was written his throne name, Nebkheperure. Herbert Winlock, an American Egyptologist, suggested that this cache, which also included animal bones, floral collars, and bags of natron (the salt used for mummification), could be the leftovers of the king's funerary feast.

Davis's disinterest in academic publishing was at odds with Ayrton's scholarly and methodical ethics. They terminated their partnership, and Davis replaced Ayrton with yet another Egyptologist, Ernest Harold Jones. Jones's major discovery was the so-called Chariot Tomb, KV58. Consisting of a single small chamber at the bottom of a shaft, this tomb yielded pieces of sheet gold, decorated with scenes and inscriptions that had once ornamented a chariot. The texts mentioned the names of Tutankhamun, as well as that of his successor, Ay. Davis declared KV58 to be the tomb of Tutankhamun. The generally accepted notion at the time was that Horemheb had destroyed Tutankhamun's proper tomb, which was supposed to lie somewhere in the vicinity of KV35, the tomb of Amenhotep II; in the chamber of KV58, which is not very far from KV35, priests faithful to Tutankhamun had hidden whatever objects they could salvage.

Davis gave up his permit to work in the Valley of the Kings in 1912, certain that the sixty-one tombs discovered by that time were all the valley had. He died three years later. Little did he know that the greatest discovery of the twentieth century was soon to happen. Davis's finds had sparked Carter's interest in discovering the tomb of the nearly forgotten king, Tutankhamun.

HOWARD CARTER OVERSEES THE REMOVAL AND PACKING OF THE WOODEN ARMCHAIR OF TUTANKHAMUN (CARTER 39) FOR TRANSPORT TO CAIRO.

HOWARD CARTER (RIGHT) WALKS WITH LORD CARNARVON IN THE VALLEY OF THE KINGS, 1922.

LORD CARNARVON OUTSIDE TUTANKHAMUN'S TOMB, HAVING JUST INSPECTED ITS CONTENTS.

MEMBERS OF THE TEAM THAT DISCOVERED THE TOMB OF TUTANKHAMUN POSE BEFORE THE ENTRANCE TO TOMB OF RAMESSES IX (KV6), IN THE VALLEY OF THE KINGS, THEBES, EGYPT. LEFT TO RIGHT: ARTHUR MACE OF THE METROPOLITAN MUSEUM, CARTER'S SECRETARY RICHARD BETHELL, ARTHUR CALLENDER, LADY EVELYN HERBERT, HOWARD CARTER, GEORGE HERBERT, FIFTH EARL OF CARNARVON WHO FINANCED THE EXCAVATION, CHEMIST ALFRED LUCAS OF THE EGYPTIAN GOVERNMENT, AND OFFICIAL PHOTOGRAPHER HARRY BURTON.

Carter did not last long in his new position as chief inspector for Lower Egypt. An incident with drunken French tourists at Saqqara in January 1905, in which Carter sided with the Egyptian guards of the site, led to his resignation only a few months after his arrival. Carter was a stubborn man, and although the head of the Antiquities Service, Gaston Maspero, wished him to return, Carter declined. He chose, instead, to support himself with the artistic talents that had first brought him to Egypt. He occasionally worked in this capacity for archaeological missions, most notably his former associate, Theodore Davis. He may also have engaged in the antiquities trade.

Maspero found an opportunity he could offer that Carter might accept in 1907. George Herbert, the Fifth Earl of Carnarvon, was coming to Egypt. Carnarvon had visited Egypt a couple of years earlier for its dry, therapeutic weather, which soothed the lingering effects of a motor vehicle accident he had suffered some years earlier. He had even undertaken some modest, and not very successful, excavations among the private tombs at Thebes.

The prospects of this collaboration brought Carter back to excavating. He joined Carnarvon's 1909 project, and the two men worked together at Luxor and elsewhere for five seasons. In 1914, in one of the major cemeteries of non-royal tombs on the Theban west bank (Dra' Abu el-Naga'), Carter found what he believed to be the tomb of the second king of the Eighteenth Dynasty, Amenhotep I, and his mother, Ahmose-Nefertari. This had been looted in antiquity, but, as in such tombs in the Valley of the Kings, much of archaeological interest remained.

With Davis out of the Valley of the Kings, the permit for excavation there was available. Carnarvon obtained it in 1914, and he and Carter began to re-excavate the long-known tomb of Amenhotep III (KV22) and to retrieve by careful excavation what ancient robbers and others had missed. The Great War interrupted their work, but Carter did manage to perform some archaeological tasks in the Valley of the Kings and elsewhere in the Theban area. With a team of hundreds, he cleared the valley to its ancient floor, hoping to locate the tomb of Tutankhamun. Discoveries were made, but nothing of great importance, and Tutankhamun eluded them completely.

The fruitlessness of the quest increasingly dissatisfied Carnarvon. In 1922, he called Carter to the family estate, Highclere Castle, to put an end to the work. Carter explained that there was an area that still required excavation. He would, if necessary, finance the project himself, and because Carnarvon was the permit holder, Carnarvon would still get his share of any finds. Carter did not need to take that drastic step. Swayed by Carter's confidence, Carnarvon agreed to extend his funding for one last season. But this time, the Earl stayed at Highclere.

Having returned to the Valley of the Kings, Carter began the work season by clearing the area that he had shown Carnarvon. The area, in front of the tomb of Ramesses V and Ramesses VI (KV9), was still crowded by the remains of the huts occupied by the workers who built this later tomb. Carter supervised the work of recording the workers' huts, photographing, documenting, and finally clearing them. He then ordered his workmen to dig through the debris on which the huts once stood, confident– hopeful—that his efforts and Carnarvon's financial investment would soon be rewarded.

HOWARD CARTER ACCOMPANIES THE GILDED WOODEN SHRINE (CARTER 108) ON ITS WAY TO THE TEMPORARY WORKROOM IN TOMB KV15 FOR ASSESSMENT AND PACKING.

HOWARD CARTER (LEFT) AND ARTHUR MACE AS THEY DISMANTLE THE DOORWAY BETWEEN THE ANTECHAMBER AND THE BURIAL CHAMBER, FEBRUARY 16, 1923.

ARTHUR CALLENDER OVERSEES THE REMOVAL OF CHARIOT PARTS AND EQUIPMENT FROM THE ANTECHAMBER, 1922.

6. THE DISCOVERY

November 4, 1922, should have been a regular day of work at the site, but as soon as he arrived on site that morning, Carter knew that something was different. By now he should have been hearing the customary singing of the workmen, but they were silent.

Their young water boy, Hussein Abdel Rassoul, ran to Carter with news. Hussein had led his jar-laden donkey onto the site earlier that morning as usual. The jars had rounded bottoms, so to stand them upright on the ground, Hussein scooped out hollows in the sand. This time, his digging had uncovered the flat surface of a stone. It was the uppermost step of a stairway leading into the ground.

By evening of the next day, Carter's workmen had cleared enough of the debris from the shaft of the stairway to reach the uppermost portion of the tomb entrance. This was blocked with stones and plaster and still retained the official necropolis seal. But Carter knew that tomb robbers had entered in antiquity. In the debris that had been excavated, it was evident that robbers had dug a tunnel that the cemetery officials had filled. And the doorway at the end of the entrance corridor had evidently been re-plastered.

Nevertheless, Carter knew he was on the cusp of a momentous discovery, even if what might wait beyond the door—sealed, broken through, and re-sealed in pharaonic times—he did not know. While there was no trace of a name among the seals that he could see on the upper part of the blocked doorway, clearly the tomb had been made for someone important.

He telegraphed Carnarvon with word of a "wonderful discovery" in the Valley of the Kings, "a magnificent tomb with seals intact."

Upon receiving this long-awaited news, Carnarvon traveled from Highclere Castle to Luxor, arriving on November 23. Carnarvon's daughter, Evelyn, caught up with them the next day. On the day of her arrival, further clearance of the doorway at last revealed a familiar and hoped-for royal name: Nebkheperure. By November 26, the doorway had been taken down, the entrance corridor beyond it was cleared, and Carter, Carnarvon, Evelyn and Carter's assistant stood before a second blocked doorway. Carter bore a hole through it.

They expected to find large furniture of the kind that Davis and Quibell had discovered in KV46, the tomb of Yuya and Tjuya. Robbers could not have removed large objects such as chairs, beds, chariots, and coffins through a narrow tunnel. But neither Carter nor Carnarvon were prepared for the "wonderful things" illuminated by their flashlight: strange human and animal figures glinting with gold, ornamented boxes, stools, chairs, and things they could not identify....

Carter and his team would spend the next ten years excavating, recording, conserving, and transporting 5,366 objects. They would find objects of gold, silver, glass, semiprecious stones, travertine, imported woods, ivory, glass, faience, linen, leather, petals, leaves, and more, all crammed into the entrance passageway and the four chambers known as the Antechamber, Burial Chamber, Treasury, and Annex. These artifacts ranged in size from the enormous shrines of gilded wood that surrounded the sarcophagus and had to be dismantled, down to tiny, individual beads. All served a specific purpose for the dead king, to help him find his way to and thrive in the netherworld—to live forever.

Most important of all, the mummy of the young golden pharaoh had remained in its nest of coffins, lying peacefully and undisturbed for more than 3,000 years.

HOWARD CARTER AND AN EGYPTIAN WORKMAN EXAMINE THE THIRD COFFIN OF TUTANKHAMUN MADE OF SOLID GOLD, INSIDE THE CASE OF THE SECOND COFFIN, OCTOBER 1925.

7. CARTER AFTER THE DISCOVERY

Carter had made the most important archaeological discovery of the twentieth century, KV62. This was a dream come true for Carter, but it was also a nightmare. The British had occupied Egypt since 1882, but Egypt's nationalistic movement was gaining momentum, and the government was interested in retaining and controlling its own ancient heritage. The law governing the divisions of archaeological finds stated that no artifacts from an intact royal tomb could leave Egypt. But was Tutankhamun's tomb, which had been robbed at least twice in antiquity, "intact"? Carter argued not, hoping to receive a percentage of the finds from the tomb for Lord Carnarvon and for himself. The Egyptian government saw the situation otherwise and insisted that the tomb was, in fact, intact, as Carter had stated at the time of his initial discovery. Nonetheless, Carter filed two lawsuits against the Egyptian government toallow the Carnarvon family to claim a share of the finds. Both failed.

HOWARD CARTER, ARTHUR CALLENDER, AND AN EGYPTIAN WORKER WRAP ONE OF THE GUARDIAN STATUES (CARTER 22) FOR TRANSPORT, NOVEMBER 29, 1923.

GUESTS GATHER FOR THE OPENING OF TUTANKHAMUN'S SEALED BURIAL CHAMBER, FEBRUARY 1923.

The efforts of colleagues and a change of government for Egypt paved the way for Carter's return to Tutankhamun's tomb in 1925. There were conditions, however. He had to work under the close supervision of the Antiquities Service, he had to permit visitors, and *The Times* of London no longer had a monopoly on the news. These were measures he had resisted before because they interfered with his scientific work, but these must have now seemed a price worth paying to complete the excavation of the tomb and the conservation and study of its objects.

The strike had occurred just as the sarcophagus had been opened: when he abandoned the tomb, Carter had literally left the stone lid hanging over the sarcophagus and the gilded outer coffin that lay within. Artifacts left in the tomb during this period of neglect had suffered. Carter's conservator, the chemist Alfred Lucas, treated them to arrest their decay. The anthropologist Douglass Derry and Professor Saleh Bey Hamdi of the Faculty of Medicine in Alexandria came to autopsy Tutankhamun's mummy in November 1925. As a professional archaeologist, Carter and his team got on with their work despite the occasional nuisances of visiting tourists and officials from the Egyptian government. He dedicated a full decade of his life to Tutankhamun and the discovery of the century.

By December 15, 1927, every object had been cleared from the tomb and cataloged. The 1927–1928 work season was taken up with photography and conservation. On January 8, 1928, the Egyptian government opened the tomb for the public to visit. The Carnarvons' involvement had ended years before, but in 1930, the late Earl's estate received £36,000 in compensation.

After finishing his work on the tomb, Carter led a quiet, struggle-free life. He published three volumes about the tomb for popular audiences, which remain in print even today, but never wrote the scholarly work he wanted to.

On March 2, 1939, Hodgkin's disease claimed his life. Some of the objects in his possession at the time of his death had come from Tutankhamun's tomb. He might have pocketed these small things before realizing that the treasures of the tomb would not be shared. Or perhaps he took them after. In any case, in recent years The Metropolitan Museum of Art has returned them to Egypt.

Nonetheless, Carter's dedication and persistence make him a role model for all archaeologists. I myself once dreamt of becoming like Carter when I was a young archaeologist. Each new generation of Egyptologists adds a fresh chapter to Carter's story. It did not end with his death.

A CROWD GROWS OUTSIDE OF TUTANKHAMUN'S TOMB, ANXIOUSLY AWAITING A GLIMPSE OF THE TREASURE, 1922.

THE SECOND COFFIN (CARTER 254) IS REMOVED FROM THE OUTERMOST COFFIN (CARTER 253) THROUGH THE USE OF A CAREFULLY ENGINEERED PULLEY SYSTEM, OCTOBER 1925.

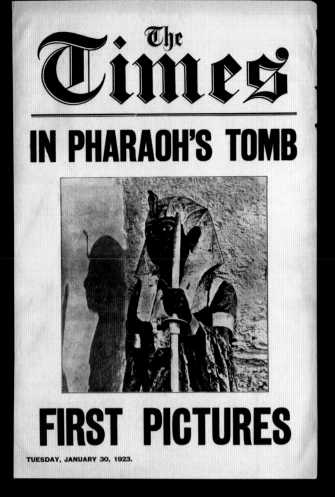

The Times

IN PHARAOH'S TOMB

FIRST PICTURES

TUESDAY, JANUARY 30, 1923.

The contract by which Carnarvon granted *The Times* of London exclusive coverage of the tomb did not prevent news of Tutankhamun's tomb from spreading around the world like wildfire. The discovery, photographs of treasures brought out from the tomb, and even Carter's strike fascinated the public. For centuries, Western civilization had been under the spell of Egyptomania, which ebbed and flowed in popularity.

In the nineteenth century, there was a great upsurge after Napoleon's scientific and military campaign in Egypt from 1798 to 1801. The result was the expansively illustrated *Description de l'Égypte,* filled with engravings of pyramids, temples, obelisks, reliefs, and all manner of antiquities that provided artists and craftsman with new inspiration. Buildings ranging from tombs to prisons to synagogues were built in the Egyptian revival style. Figures of pharaohs supported tables, sphinxes reclined on clock cases, and scenes of Egyptian fishermen adorned dinnerware. Operas with Egyptian themes, such as *Aïda*, appeared on the stage. Theodore Davis and his discoveries in the Valley of the Kings gave these an additional boost in the first two decades of the twentieth century. Carter's discovery of Tutankhamun's tomb brought a fresh wave for the 1920s. "King Tut" sold newspapers.

But *The Times*'s stranglehold was a problem, so competing papers found a "Tut" story that they could cover: the ailing Lord Carnarvon. A razor-nicked mosquito bite on his cheek had become infected, and in March 1923, he lay ill in the Continental-Savoy Hotel in Cairo. Unscrupulous writers began to spread rumors of a pharaoh's curse. These escalated with Carnarvon's death on April 5, 1923. It was alleged that Tutankhamun's mummy had a wound on the same part of the face as Carnarvon's mosquito bite. A power outage in Cairo, a snake eating

A POSTCARD FOR THE CONTINENTAL-SAVOY HOTEL IN CAIRO, WHERE LORD CARNARVON SPENT HIS FINAL DAYS.

LORD CARNARVON RELAXES AT HOWARD CARTER'S HOME ON THE THEBAN WEST BANK.

Carter's pet canary, the deaths of anyone who had visited the tomb, and much else were attributed to the supernatural powers of the ancient Egyptians.

But such powers were fictions, and the tales, some spun from real events, followed a tradition of mummy stories that can be easily traced back to the nineteenth century and perhaps even earlier. These often involve curses that take a toll on some unfortunate visitor who enters a tomb or otherwise disturbs the ancient dead.

The Egyptians really did protect their tombs with what might today be called curses. These warn the violator that they might suffer anything from loss of social status to oblivion in the afterlife. Carter found a clay brick with a protective text written on it, but this was a far cry from a curse. It reads, in part, "I am the one [...] who would repel him with the desert flame. [...] I have caused the path to be mistaken." This was reported in the press as a threat to kill all who enter the tomb. The press also concocted a false story that one of the golden shrines erected around the sarcophagus promised that a swift-winged death would befall all who entered the pharaoh's final resting place.

The story of the curse has remained alive all these years. Each traveling Tutankhamun exhibit seemed to invite more manifestations of the "curse." An Antiquities Service official who was struck and killed crossing a busy Cairo street was named a victim because he had signed the contract for one of the exhibitions. When famed Egyptian actor Omar Sharif lost a lawsuit in Los Angeles, that was blamed on Tut's curse because an exhibit had been shown in L.A. When I called upon the president of the Exelon Corporation—one of the corporate sponsors of the Tutankhamun exhibit in Chicago in 2006—to donate an Egyptian coffin he owned to the Field Museum, his reluctance to provide it was blamed on the pharaoh's curse.

I myself have experienced things that might seem like a curse from the boy king. When my team headed to the Valley of the Kings to perform CAT scans on his mummy, our driver nearly ran over a child. En route, we received news that the minister of culture, Farouk Hosni, had had a heart attack. A rainstorm struck the area after a Japanese news crew interviewed me. And, the next morning, the CAT scanner refused to work.

Although, for a moment, even I had to wonder whether there might be a curse, rational thought makes one realize that these are all coincidences. (We solved the problem of the CAT scanner by cooling the equipment with a fan. If an electric fan is all that is needed to break a pharaoh's curse, it is a very weak curse indeed!) Many of Carter's team members lived long lives. Carnarvon's daughter, Evelyn, who sneaked into the tomb with Carter and may even have been in love with him, lived until 1980, dying at the age of seventy-nine. Alan Gardiner, an expert in the ancient language, lived forty-one years after the tomb's discovery. Even Carter himself, who should have been the prime target of a curse, was a respectable sixty-four when he died.

Of all the results of Egyptomania, the most important is Egyptology itself. It developed as an academic discipline while people were lining their living rooms with lotus-patterned wallpaper. The Tutmania of the twentieth and, now, the twenty-first centuries will keep Egyptology alive. The beauty and mysteries that objects from the tomb still hold will inspire fascination, appreciation, and understanding.

These are the real treasures of Tutankhamun.

INLAID WOODEN CARTOUCHE BOX

Carter 269 / JE 61490 / GEM 242
Coniferous wood, ebony, ivory, gesso, gilding, paint
Length 64 cm; width 30.7 cm; height 33.2 cm
Found on the floor of the Treasury

The ancient craftsman created this box in the shape of a cartouche, a symbolic oval of rope in which the king's birth name and his throne name were written. It was related to the round *shen* ring, a sign for "eternity," and was a protective sign. The signs that were carved in ebony and ivory and applied to the upper surface of the lid spell out Tutankhamun's birth name. The god Amun's name, written with a reed leaf, a game board, and a water sign, appears first. The two loaves of bread (half circles) and the quail chick between them form *tut*, meaning "image." The *ankh*, so familiar even in modern times, means "life." The next three signs are his epithet. The first, a scepter in the form of a shepherd's crook, is *heqa*, ("ruler"). The next sign represents the city of Heliopolis, an important center of Re's cult in the north. The last sign, the sedge plant (*shemu*), means "Upper Egyptian"

or "southern." These may be translated as "ruler of Southern Heliopolis," or "ruler of Thebes." Thebes was considered to be the Upper Egyptian equivalent of Re's city in the north.

The craftsman stained parts of the ivory. The resulting polychrome effect stands out crisply against the gilded background. An inscription carved into the rope of the cartouche gives more of the king's many formal names and epithets. The box has two knobs, one on the lid and one on the corresponding side. It would be closed with twine, which could then be secured with a daub of wax and impressed with a seal. The god Heh ("Eternity") appears on the knobs.

Names were important to the Egyptians. They were aspects of the self and were necessary for survival in the netherworld. Changing Tutankhaten's name to Tutankhamun, would have been a serious decision, not taken lightly.

WOODEN ARMCHAIR OF TUTANKHAMUN

Carter 39 / JE 62033 / GEM 378
Ebony, ivory, gesso, gold leaf
Height 71.5 cm; width 40.6 cm; depth 39.1 cm
Found beneath a lion-shaped ritual bed in the Antechamber

This little chair was made for Tutankhamun while he was still a young boy. It has no inscriptions, but its beauty and the quality of its materials demonstrate that it was created for a member of the royal family. The legs are in the form of a lion's legs, a popular design element for ancient Egyptian furniture, as are the vertical and diagonal supports and the horizontal stretchers between the legs. The contrasting inlays of ebony and ivory are also very Egyptian. But Tutankhamun ruled in an age of intense artistic influences and exchanges among Egypt and its neighbors. Each arm has two panels of carved and gilded decoration that took inspiration from styles in use in the Aegean and in Syria. On the inner panels, a stylized desert plant grows out to fill the space. On each outer panel, a reclining ibex turns its head to look behind and bleat. Perhaps it is hiding in the plants that surround it. A scrolling wave frames the image.

GILDED WOODEN SHRINE

Carter 108 / JE 61481 / GEM 199-1
Wood, gesso, gold leaf, silver
Height 50.5 cm; width 30.7 cm; depth 48 cm
Found in the Antechamber

The scenes carved into the wood of this little shrine show Ankhesenamun attending her husband, Tutankhamun. The small scenes on the two doors on the front of the shrine show her venerating the king with raised hands, shaking a ceremonial rattle before him, offering him bunches of flowers, and supporting him as he walks. Similar scenes appear at a larger scale on the left side and on the back. She pours water or wine into a chalice, places a necklace upon him, offers him the notched palm ribs that signify an eternal reign, and performs other ritual acts. Once, she receives something from him: Tutankhamun pours oil into his wife's cupped hand. On the right side are three somewhat different images of the king and queen. In one, she helps him walk, an act that appears also on the door, but the other two scenes show bird

He prepares to throw a boomerang into the marshes. In the other, the king sits in a chair and aims an arrow at his target. Seated on the ground, Ankhesenamun is ready with another for his next shot.

The actions and the queen's costumes indicate that these scenes are sexual in nature, although this may not be obvious to the modern viewer. Ankhesenamun's crowns and some of the objects she holds relate her to the goddess of love and sex, Hathor. The texts refer to a serpent goddess named Weret-hekau, "Great of Magic," who suckled the king. All of the queen's actions may help the king achieve rebirth in the netherworld, and the shrine may have played a role in rituals during the king's lifetime as well. Within it was a pedestal where a figure of a god or the king may have stood, but the figure was missing. Although these scenes are stylized and ritualized, they appear to reflect genuine affection between the

GILDED WOODEN STATUE OF HERWER (HORUS THE ELDER)

Carter 293-a(a) / JE 60746 / GEM 91
Wood, gesso, gold leaf, black resin, copper alloy, obsidian, glass
Height (overall) 56.8 cm; length (pedestal) 21 cm; width (pedestal) 12.5 cm
Found in a wooden box in the form of a shrine in the Treasury

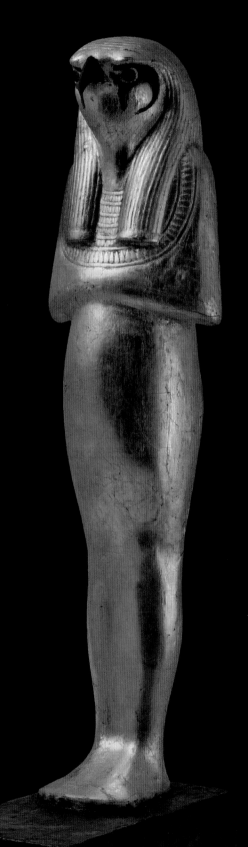

The falcon-headed deity is Horus the Elder, Herwer. Horus was a god worshipped throughout Egypt, and he had several different forms. As Horakhty ("Horus of the Two Horizons") or Horemakhet ("Horus in the Horizon"), he was the powerful sun god. As Harsiesis ("Horus, Son of Isis") or Harpocrates ("Horus the Child"), he was the vulnerable child of the goddess Isis and her husband, Osiris. One of the most important myths of ancient Egypt was the story of Osiris. The eldest son of the earth god Geb, he was his father's appointed heir to the throne. His envious younger brother, Seth, slew Osiris, scattered the parts of the corpse, and usurped the throne. Isis bound up Osiris's body and brought him back to life. They conceived a son, Horus, before Osiris descended to the netherworld to reign as king of the dead. Seth never managed to capture his young nephew, who grew up to do battle with him. Horus emerged victorious and inherited his father's throne. Horus was closely identified with the king.

36

GILDED WOODEN STATUE OF PTAH

Carter 291-a(a) / JE 60739 / GEM 109
Wood, gesso, gold leaf, black resin, faience, glass
Height (overall) 60 cm; length (pedestal) 26 cm; width (pedestal) 7.4 cm
Found in a wooden box in the form of a shrine in the Treasury

Readily recognizable by his mummy shape and blue skullcap, Ptah was the creator god worshipped at Memphis. He holds in his hands a scepter combining the signs for "dominion," "life," and "stability." According to the Memphite creation myth, the universe came into being because of his thought and spoken word. He was worshipped as a god of craftsmen. Carvings of his ears were created so that people could pray directly to him in their time of need.

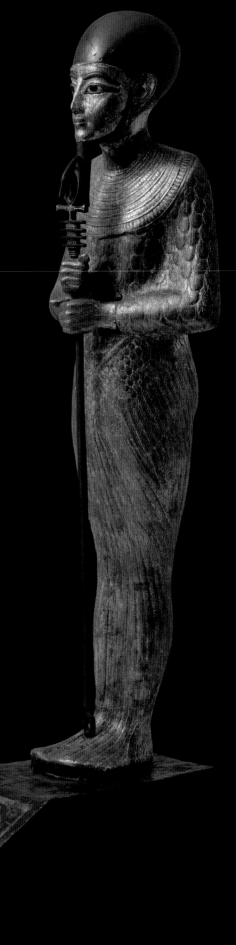

WOODEN CEREMONIAL SHIELD WITH KING AS SPHINX

Carter 379-a / JE 61577
Wood, stucco, gold leaf, ebony
Height 89.5 cm; width 54 cm; thickness 1.0 cm
Found under a wooden bed in the Annex

The ornate openwork of this wooden shield would have provided no protection on the battlefield. It was intended for ceremonial or ritual occasions. Tutankhamun appears as a striding sphinx, a human-headed lion. The fan beside him is a mark of royalty. The falcon perched on it may be Montu, a war god whose cult center was at Thebes. Overhead, the sun disk spreads its wings protectively above the king. Tutankhamun wears two headdresses: the striped *nemes* headdress (which appears on his golden mask) and the double crown of a united Egypt.

His paws trample two foreign foes, a pair of Nubians. One of them raises his hand helplessly. Below these men is the hieroglyphic sign for "foreign land." This was one of the many ways that the Egyptians expressed their idea that the entire world belonged to the pharaoh.

PECTORAL, CHAIN, AND COUNTERPOISE WITH LAPIS SCARAB FLANKED BY URAEI

Carter 267-g, -h / JE 61896 / GEM 142
Gold, silver, carnelian turquoise, lapis lazuli, green feldspar, glass
Length 50 cm
Found in a box made of ivory and ebony in the Treasury

Solar imagery abounds on objects from the tomb, not surprisingly, given that even before the "heresy" of Akhenaten, the sun god dominated Egyptian religion. Scarabs carved of lapis lazuli, a highly prized dark blue stone found in Afghanistan, form the central motif of the pectoral and its massive straps. The scarab, a kind of beetle, represented Khepri, the sun god in the morning, pushing the disk of the sun over the horizon. The beetle lays its eggs in a ball of dung and rolls it along the ground. Seeing beetles crawling out of dung gave the Egyptians the idea to use such an image to signify eternal rebirth of the sun and, therefore, of the individual in the afterlife. The scarab was used to write the word for "becoming" or "form" (*kheper*),

an element of Tutankhamun's throne name. Khepri appears here in a solar barque. On either side is one of the sun god's guardians, the uraeus or divine cobra. Each has a solar disk on its head.

The ornamentation of the straps consists of repeated writings of Nebkheperure: the scarab (*kheper*) on a basket (*neb*), and, above the scarab, a solar disk (*re*) with uraei. This combination of signs alternates with pairs of uraei. At the other end of each strap is a vulture with outspread wings, a symbol of the goddess Nekhbet, patron goddess of Upper Egypt. Attached to the pair of vultures are strings of beads from which hang a pair of cobras, face to face. These may represent Nekhbet's Lower Egyptian counterpart, the goddess Wadjet.

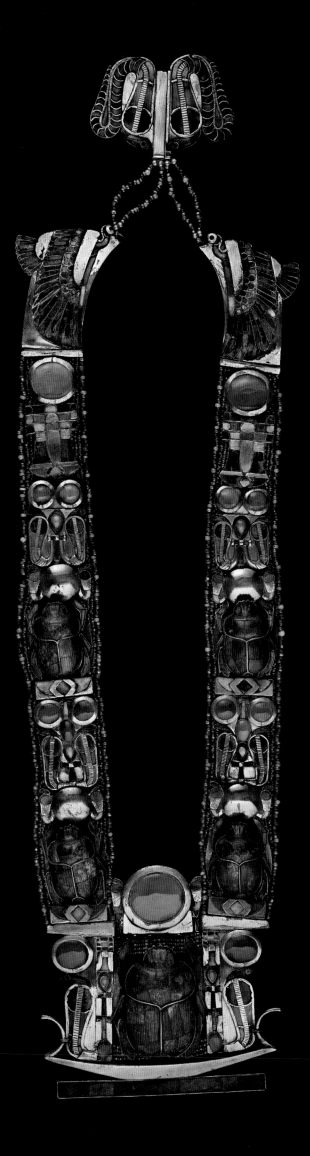

PECTORAL IN THE FORM OF A GOLD BOAT AND SILVER SOLAR DISK

Carter 269-k / JE 61897 / GEM 139
Gold, electrum, lapis lazuli, green feldspar, travertine, glass, resin, carnelian
Maximum height (pectoral) 11.8 cm; maximum width (pectoral) 10.8 cm; length (chains)
23.5 cm; maximum height (counterpoise) 6.2 cm; maximum width (counterpoise) 6.8 cm
Found in the cartouche-shaped box in the Treasury

Inspired by the Nile River, the Egyptians portrayed the sun (p. 38) and the moon traveling across the heavens in boats. The pectoral of this necklace depicts the lunar barque, which can be distinguished from the solar boat by the silver color of its disk and by the crescent below it. The silver-colored metal used here is electrum, an alloy of silver and gold. The barque sails across a celestial marsh represented by lotus blossoms growing out of the hieroglyphic sign for "sky." Another, much larger lotus flower with rosettes at its base serves as the counterpoise. From this hang tassels of small beads.

Larger beads form the chain that connects the counterpoise and pectoral. These are made of alternating bands of barrel beads and spherical beads made of gold, semiprecious stones, and resin.

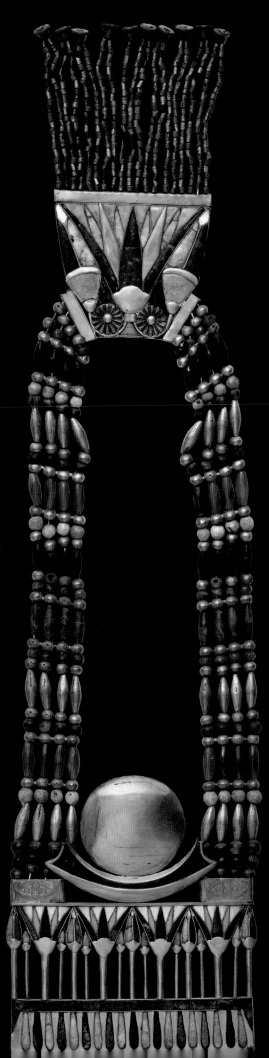

GOLD INLAID VULTURE PECTORAL, CHAIN, AND COUNTERPOISE

Carter 256-ppp / JE 61892 / GEM 137
Gold, lapis lazuli, turquoise, carnelian, glass
Maximum height (pendant) 6.5 cm; maximum width (pendant) 11.0 cm
Found in the Burial Chamber among the wrappings of the mummy

The vulture deity represented by this pendant is Nekhbet, patron goddess of Upper Egypt. Although the body and feathers are highly stylized in form and color, the goddess's head has been realistically modeled by an artist familiar with the living bird. The goddess's claws grasp *shen* signs and around her neck is the image of a tiny necklace with the king's throne name.

The elements of the chain are gold and lapis lazuli with little glass beads. The slide clasp is in the form of two falcons.

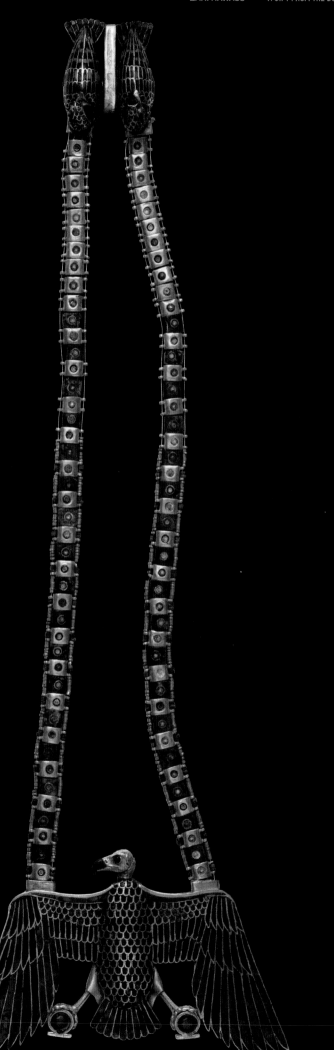

GOLD INLAID FALCON PECTORAL WITH HEART-SHAPED COUNTERPOISE AND CHAIN

Carter 256-uuu / JE 61891 / GEM 500
Gold, chalcedony, glass, carnelian, lapis lazuli
Height (pectoral) 8.5 cm; width (pectoral) 9 cm; length (chain) 65 cm; length (counterpoise) 3.5 cm
Found in the Burial Chamber among the wrappings of the mummy

Birds with outspread and often upswept wings are common in Egyptian art, but most have their heads turned to one side (p. 41, 45). The craftsman of this outstanding example has faced the falcon forward to stare directly at the viewer. The wings are inlaid in the conventional manner, but the body is a gold "cage" for a green stone, thought to be chalcedony.

The bird, representing the sun god Re-Horakhty, carries a *shen* sign in each claw, and on its head is a large solar disk formed with a piece of polished carnelian.

The chain, made of braided goldwire, ends in two round carnelian beads and a counterpoise in the shape of a heart. This has the king's throne name, Nebkheperure, colorfully inlaid.

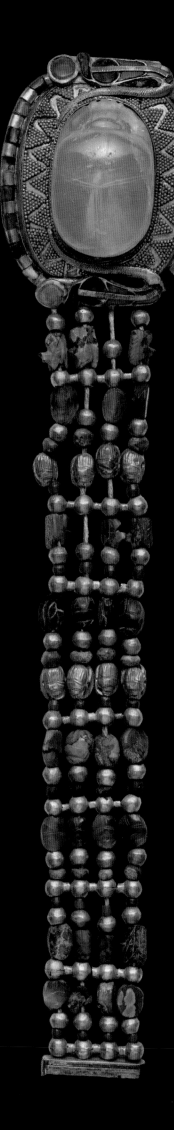

GOLD, LAPIS, AND CARNELIAN BEAD BRACELET WITH AMETHYST SCARAB CLASP

Carter 269-m / JE 62380 / GEM 10749
Gold, amethyst, lapis lazuli, turquoise, carnelian, red jasper, glass
Length (band) 13.5 cm; width (band) 1.9 cm;
length (centerpiece) 4.5 cm; width (centerpiece) 4.1 cm
Found in the cartouche-shaped box in the Treasury

The translucent purple stone used for the scarab of this bracelet is amethyst, a stone mined in the Eastern Desert. The height of its appeal to the Egyptians was during the Middle Kingdom, centuries before Tutankhamun's reign, by which time its use was much less common. The scarab is set into an oval bezel decorated with gold granulation. Divine cobras, like the scarab associated with the sun, guard each end. Four strands of beads form the band. The blue beads are lapis lazuli, and the red beads are carnelian and jasper, and there is one red glass bead as well.

On the back of the bezel is Tutankhamun's throne name, Nebkheperure.

WESEKH COLLAR-SHAPED EARRING WITH BLUE GLASS DUCK

Carter 269-a(1) / JE 61969-a / GEM 485-a
Gold, quartz, travertine, faience, glass
Length 10.9 cm; width 5.2 cm
Found in a small box inside the cartouche-shaped
box in the Treasury

This earring, one of a pair, may have been made for Tutankhamun when he was very young. The general design of the body and wings of the bird is much like that of the Gold Inlaid Falcon Pectoral (p. 42). However, the head, made of deep blue glass, is not that of a falcon. It is a duck. Clearly the craftsman, and whoever commissioned the piece, had a sense of whimsy. From the tail of this charming hybrid bird hangs an element that terminates in five uraei. Just above where the wings of the bird meet is a design reminiscent of a broad collar. The button that caps the stud of the earring is a clear glass dome that covers a gold disk. This is guarded by two more uraei.

ACELET DECORATED
EEN STONE

66 / GEM 3317
se
maximum diameter 5.5 cm
mber on the left arm of
e wrappings

f pale, veined stone, probably turquoise, forms
his bracelet. The plain surface of the stone
nse geometric patterns and waves formed by
granules of gold, small gold hemispheres, and
hank of this bracelet consists of three tubes
es of electrum, with ends given the form of

mined in the Eastern Desert and in the Sinai
e associated with Hathor, goddess of love, who
s of Turquoise.

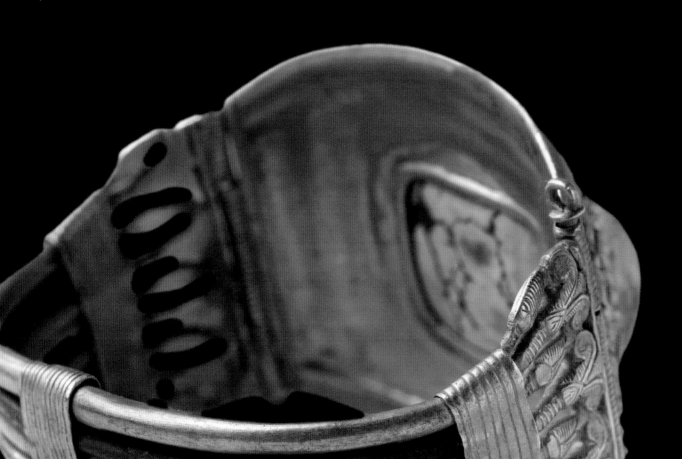

GILDED WOODEN "OSTRICH HUNT" FAN

Carter 242 / JE 62001 / GEM 284
Wood, gold leaf
Length (overall) 105.5 cm; width (fan) 18.5 cm
Found on the floor between the third and fourth shrines
surrounding the sarcophagus in the Burial Chamber

Each side of this fan presents an episode of a hunt not unlike that on the bow case (p. 54), but here his quarry is specifically ostriches. On one side, as hunting dogs run along with the horses pulling his chariot, Tutankhamun draws his bow to shoot an arrow at the huge birds. One has already fallen victim to his sharp aim. The scene on the other side shows the king's fruitful return, with the dead ostriches being carried by men in his retinue. In both scenes the king is accompanied by an anthropomorphic *ankh* ("life") sign, which holds a fan to give the king shade and a cool breeze. According to the inscription on the stock of the fan, the king himself had provided its feathers, which came from a successful hunt near Heliopolis, in Lower Egypt (near Cairo). When Carter found this fan in the king's Burial Chamber, the feathers had all but disintegrated.

GILDED WOODEN COMPOUND BOW WITH GLASS AND CALCITE INLAY

Carter 48-h / JE 61517 / GEM 4860
Wood, gold, glass (presumably also horn, sinew)
Length 133 cm
Found bundled with staves and bows
in the Antechamber

The bow was a weapon of great antiquity, and both the Egyptians and the Nubians had expert archers among their fighting forces. But bow-makers in Asia had improved the weapon by combining wood, horn, and sinew into what is known as a composite bow, which gave the arrow shot from such a bow a greater range.

Tutankhamun had more than thirty composite bows, along with forty-seven of the older style (self bow), and more than four hundred arrows.

Near the center of the bow, where it would be gripped, are bands inscribed in gold with Tutankhamun's throne name, Nebkheperure. Gold wire, sheet gold, and colorful glass inlay ornament this extremely elaborate weapon. Despite all of this embellishment, it is a working bow, which the king may have used during his lifetime.

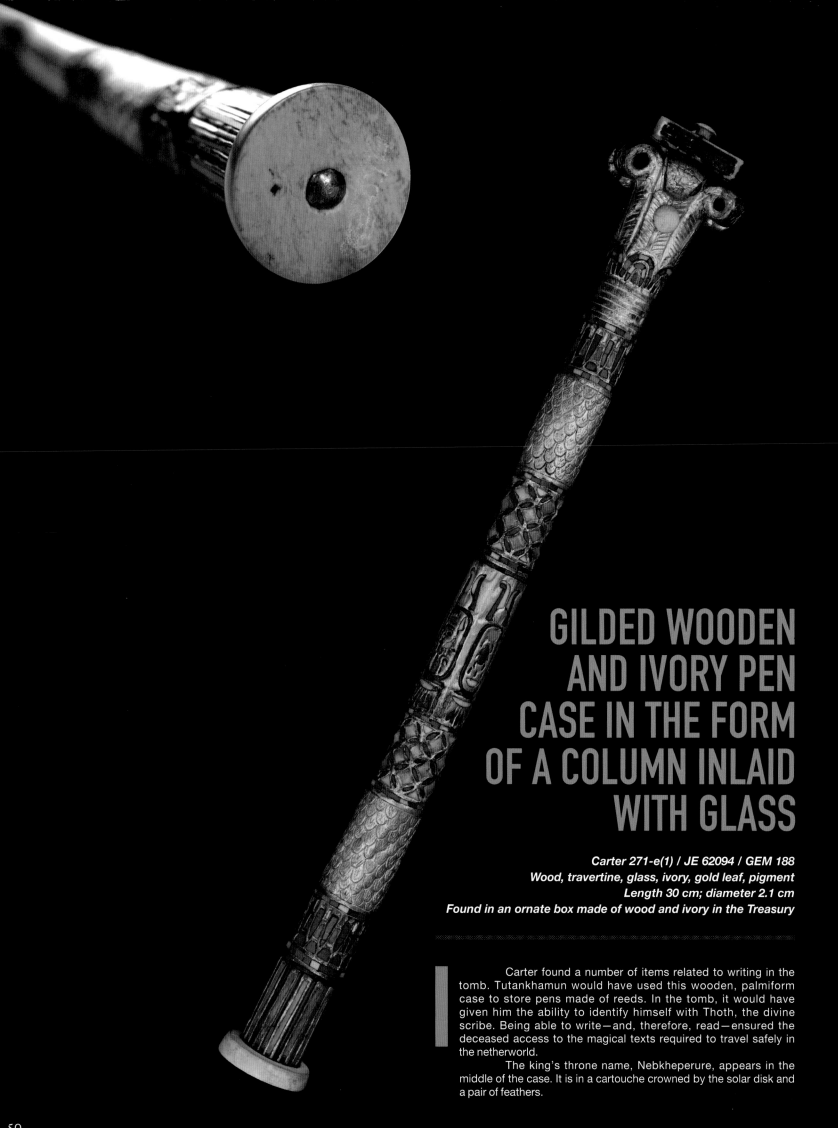

GILDED WOODEN AND IVORY PEN CASE IN THE FORM OF A COLUMN INLAID WITH GLASS

Carter 271-e(1) / JE 62094 / GEM 188
Wood, travertine, glass, ivory, gold leaf, pigment
Length 30 cm; diameter 2.1 cm
Found in an ornate box made of wood and ivory in the Treasury

Carter found a number of items related to writing in the tomb. Tutankhamun would have used this wooden, palmiform case to store pens made of reeds. In the tomb, it would have given him the ability to identify himself with Thoth, the divine scribe. Being able to write—and, therefore, read—ensured the deceased access to the magical texts required to travel safely in the netherworld.

The king's throne name, Nebkheperure, appears in the middle of the case. It is in a cartouche crowned by the solar disk and a pair of feathers.

RED WOODEN SEMICIRCULAR BOX AND INLAID LID

Carter 79, 574 / JE 61495.1–2 / GEM 12720.1–2
Ebony, coniferous wood, gold leaf, ivory,
gesso, paint, resin
Height 37.5 cm; depth 31 cm
Found on a ritual bed in the form of a
cow in the Antechamber (box)
and on the floor of the Annex (lid)

This box may have been used during the king's lifetime to transport documents written on papyrus. Its metal loops would have made it easy to carry. The court was often on the move, as the king traveled from one royal duty to another—often a religious festival. On the front of the box is the *sema-tawy* sign, a combination of human lungs and windpipe around which the heraldic plants of Upper and Lower Egypt intertwine, signifying the "union of the Two Lands."

It was not originally made for Tutankhamun although the three cartouches below the ebony knob on the front give his two names and the name of Ankhesenamun. These are alterations. The original inscription gave the names of Tutankhamun's predecessor, Ankhkheperure, and eldest half-sister, Meritaten.

No other box of this shape is known from ancient Egypt.

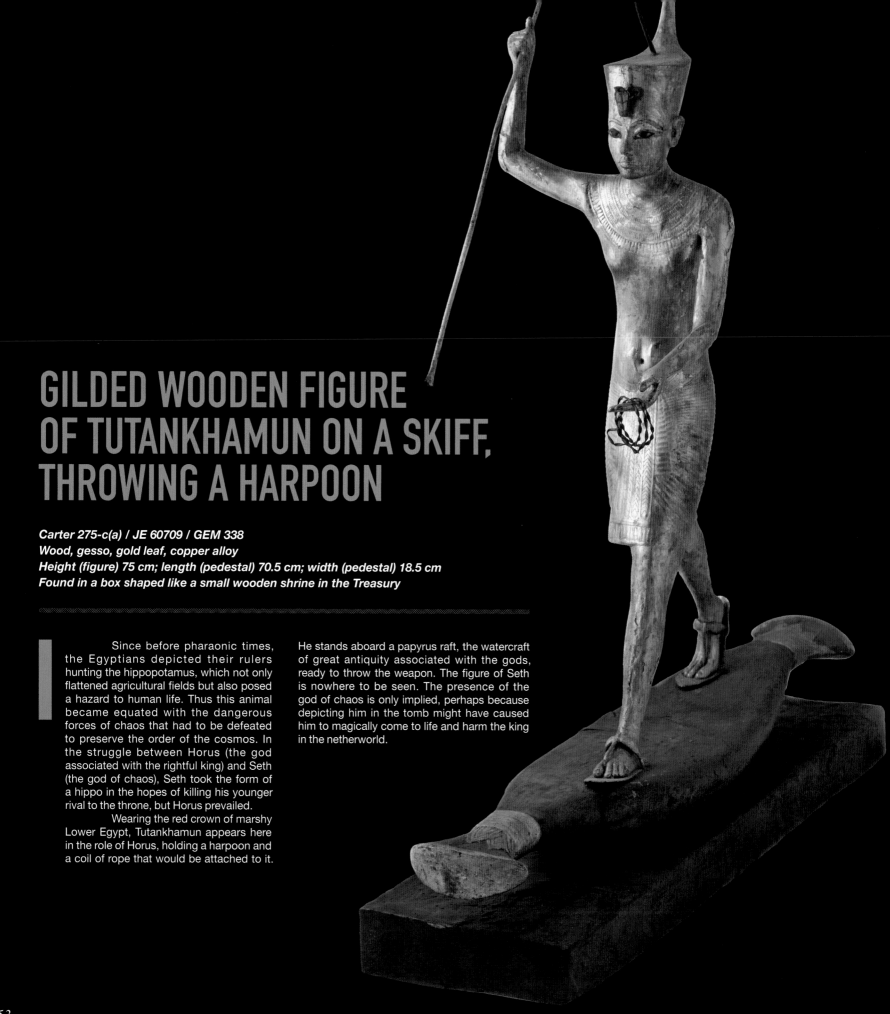

GILDED WOODEN FIGURE OF TUTANKHAMUN ON A SKIFF, THROWING A HARPOON

Carter 275-c(a) / JE 60709 / GEM 338
Wood, gesso, gold leaf, copper alloy
Height (figure) 75 cm; length (pedestal) 70.5 cm; width (pedestal) 18.5 cm
Found in a box shaped like a small wooden shrine in the Treasury

Since before pharaonic times, the Egyptians depicted their rulers hunting the hippopotamus, which not only flattened agricultural fields but also posed a hazard to human life. Thus this animal became equated with the dangerous forces of chaos that had to be defeated to preserve the order of the cosmos. In the struggle between Horus (the god associated with the rightful king) and Seth (the god of chaos), Seth took the form of a hippo in the hopes of killing his younger rival to the throne, but Horus prevailed.

Wearing the red crown of marshy Lower Egypt, Tutankhamun appears here in the role of Horus, holding a harpoon and a coil of rope that would be attached to it.

He stands aboard a papyrus raft, the watercraft of great antiquity associated with the gods, ready to throw the weapon. The figure of Seth is nowhere to be seen. The presence of the god of chaos is only implied, perhaps because depicting him in the tomb might have caused him to magically come to life and harm the king in the netherworld.

GILDED BOW CASE WITH SCENES OF TUTANKHAMUN HUNTING FROM A CHARIOT

Carter 335 / JE 61502 / GEM 367
Wood, copper, linen, plaster, bark, leather, faience, beetle wings
Length 153 cm; maximum width 25 cm; thickness 7 cm
Found standing in the northwest corner of the Treasury

Tutankhamun would have kept his bows, such as that on p. 49, in this case. The head of a lion, modeled in faience, caps each end. Carving and inlays of various materials provide geometric and floral designs, inscriptions, figures, and scenes. Near the ends are images of the king as a sphinx or a lion trampling foreign foes.

Many images in the tomb present Tutankhamun playing the role of warrior or hunter in obviously symbolic contexts (p. 37), but some, such as the bow case and one of the fans (p. 48) present more realistic scenarios. In the center on each side of this case, the king in his chariot, in the company of his hunting dogs, pursues hyenas, gazelles, oryxes, hare, and other animals of the desert, which fall prey to his arrows.

INLAID GOLD HANDS HOLDING THE CROOK AND FLAIL

Carter 256-b(1) / JE 606739c / GEM 759-A, J
Gold, carnelian, glass, silver
Found on the wrapped mummy in the Burial Chamber

Gold hands were sewn onto the mummy wrappings at the chest. Holding two ancient symbols of kingship, the crook and flail, these add to the appearance of the king as the god Osiris, king of the netherworld, who also appears grasping these scepters. The crook and flail are silver (a metal scarcer and thus more valuable than in Egypt at this time) covered with gold and glass. From the end of the flail hang beads of glass, carnelian, and gold.

EXTERNAL TRAPPINGS OF THE MUMMY

PECTORAL IN THE FORM OF A *NAOS* WITH WINGED FELDSPAR SCARAB

Carter 256-b / JE 61902-a / GEM 759-A, J
Resin, gold, faience
Width 4.8 cm; length 6 cm
Found on the mummy in the Burial Chamber

The king's golden mask (Carter 256a) may be the most famous of the objects that Carter found on the outer wrappings of Tutankhamun's mummy, but it was only one of many crucial fittings.

The bands from which the scarab hangs were made for Ankhkheperure. The scarab itself, carved from resin, has on its base a spell from the Book of the Dead.

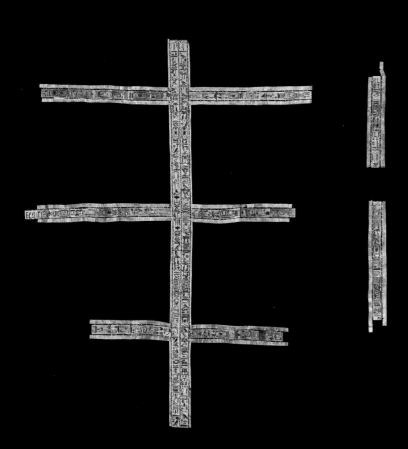

TWO VERTICAL SIDE STRAPS

Carter 256-b(4) / JE 60673b, JE 60673b(b) / GEM 759-A, J
Gold, carnelian, glass, faience
Found on the wrapped
mummy in the Burial Chamber

FOUR HORIZONTAL AND TWO VERTICAL GOLD MUMMY BANDS

Carter no. 256-b(3) / JE 60683(a), JE 61902-b(a) / GEM 759-A, J
Gold, carnelian, lapis lazuli, faience, feldspar
Found on the wrapped mummy in the Burial Chamber

A mummy of lesser stature than Tutankhamun's would have had straps and bands such as these made of linen. But Tutankhamun's are gold embellished with inlays that provide the king's name and spells spoken by deities who guard the king, including the jackal god Anubis, the sky goddess Nut, and the four sons of Horus, protectors of the internal organs removed and preserved separately during the mummification process.

The undersides of the bands are also inscribed. Carter noticed that almost everywhere that there had been a cartouche on the underside, it had been cut out and replaced with a piece of plain gold. But the craftsmen had missed one, so it is known that these mummy bands were originally created for Tutankhamun's predecessor, Ankhkheperure. Quite a number of objects in Tutankhamun's tomb had been intended for her, including the scarab (p. 56) and the statuette of the king on a black leopard (p. 61).

GOLD *BA* BIRD PECTORAL WITH GLASS INLAYS

Carter 256-b(2) / JE 61903 / GEM 759-A, J
Gold, glass
Height 12.5 cm; width 33 cm
Thebes, Valley of the Kings, KV62,
Burial Chamber

If properly equipped with spells, a person's *ba* (a word often translated as "soul") was thought to be able to fly out of the tomb by day. For this reason, the Egyptians envisioned a *ba* as a human-headed bird. Like other images of divine birds (p. 41, 45, 48), the wings, body, and tail are colorfully inlaid and the talons hold the hieroglyphic sign for "eternity." The *ba*'s sensitively rendered human face is that of the king wearing a diadem similar to one found on the mummy.

SHABTIS:
SERVANTS FOR THE AFTERLIFE

WOODEN *SHABTI* IN EBONY *KHEPRESH* CROWN

Carter 318-a / JE 60830 / GEM 174
Wood, gold leaf, paint
Height 48 cm
Found in a shrine-shaped box in the Treasury

The *khepresh* or blue crown— sometimes called the "war crown"—worn by this *shabti* is made of ebony. The band and uraeus on the crown and the broad collar that drapes his chest have been brightened with gold leaf. Paint provides his eyes and eyebrows, and his lips have been colored pink. The craftsman who carved the king's figure even gave him pierced ears, which the king had in life. This figure was a gift from one of Tutankhamun's courtiers, a general named Nakhtmin who, some think, might have been the son of Tutankhamun's successor, Ay.

The ancient Egyptian netherworld, or *Duat*, in some respects resembled the world of the living. There were fields, farms, waterways, and even towns. The dead ate, drank, and enjoyed their leisure much as the living did. But this meant that there was work to be done, too, particularly agricultural chores. The Egyptians devised a way to avoid the unpleasant tasks that the gods might call on them to accomplish. They created servant figures, usually called *shabtis*, and a spell that would "activate" them: "I will do it. Here I am!" the *shabti* would reply and go off to do the work.

Because even kings were not immune to such calls for labor, Tutankhamun has a large enough workforce to provide a servant figure for each day of the year, plus an overseer for every ten workers, and a supervisor for every three overseers. His hundreds of figures vary greatly in detail, material, and craftsmanship.

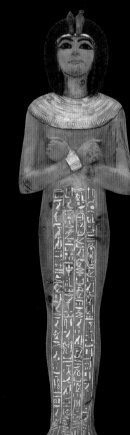

WOODEN *SHABTI* IN ROUND EBONY WIG

Carter 326-a-1 / JE 60835 / GEM 39126
Wood, copper alloy, gilding, paint
Height 54 cm
Found in a shrine-shaped box in the Treasury

This *shabti* wears a fashionable hairstyle known as the Nubian wig. A round wig of tight curls, inspired by the hairstyle of Nubian mercenaries who served in the Egyptian army, it was popular among men and women during this period. Again, details of the king's costume are highlighted with gold. This figure and the one above grasp the crook and flail of kingship, symbols associated with the mummiform ruler of the dead, Osiris.

WOODEN GUARDIAN STATUE OF THE *KA* OF THE KING

Carter 22 / JE 60707 / GEM 5
Wood, bitumen, gesso, gilding, copper alloy, limestone, obsidian
Height 190 cm; width 56 cm; width (base) 33.5 cm
Found in the Antechamber, standing beside the wall
between the Antechamber and the Burial Chamber

When Carter and Carnarvon entered the first room (Antechamber) of Tutankhamun's tomb, they encountered this life-size figure of the king beside a wall, facing another figure very similar to it. Carter would discover that they were standing guard on either side of the bricked-up and plastered-over entrance to the Burial Chamber. The skin of this figure, like its counterpart, is painted with black bitumen, the color of fertility and rebirth. Its clothing, jewelry and other objects are gilded. The craftsman made the eyes of the king from white limestone with irises of obsidian set into gold frames.

The king, who wears an elaborate kilt with a stiff, triangular apron, takes a forceful stride. In his right hand he grasps one of Egypt's most ancient weapons, a mace with a stone head. In his left, he holds a staff called the *mekes*, which also might have been a weapon in Egypt's most ancient history. On his head is the striped cloth known as the *nemes*, a headdress that associates him with the god Horus and with the morning sun. Appropriately, this figure stood on the eastern side of the Burial Chamber entrance. An inscription reads, "The good god to whom one bows, the sovereign of whom one boasts, Nebkheperure, son of Re, lord of diadems, Tutankhamun ruler in Southern Heliopolis (Thebes), living forever like Re, every day." Its counterpart, which stood on the western side, has attributes that associate it with the sun at night and with the netherworld.

The guardian statues (as they are known in modern times) magically protected the entrance to the Burial Chamber and the king's all-important mummy from harm.

"WISHING CUP" IN THE FORM OF AN OPEN LOTUS FLOWER AND TWO BUDS

Carter 14, 24-xxx / JE 62125 / GEM 36
Travertine, paint
Height 18 cm; width (handles) 30 cm;
diameter (cup) 17 cm
Found inside the blocking of
the inner doorway to the Antechamber

This drinking cup takes the form of an open white lotus flower (*Nymphaea lotus*) with flowers and closed buds of the blue lotus (*Nymphaea cerulea*) forming the handles on either side. The blue lotus, which opens at dawn, is thought to have emerged from the primordial waters and opened up to reveal the sun in the moment of creation. Blossoms of the white lotus open at night, associating it with the moon and the sun.

Atop each blue lotus flower is a basket, symbolizing "all," on which kneels Heh, the god of eternity. As seen on other pieces in the tomb, Heh holds a palm rib with a tadpole. These signs, taken together, signify a reign of 100,000 years. The sign of life (*ankh*) appears here as well.

The inscriptions on the two sides of the cup give the names of the king and his titles. Drinking from a cup such as this was a way to magically achieve eternal contentedness. Around the rim, the hieroglyphic signs proclaim a well wish for the king's *ka* (his life force, which persisted after death).

GILDED WOODEN STATUETTE OF TUTANKHAMUN RIDING A LEOPARD

Carter 289-b / JE 60714 / GEM 11552
Wood, gilding, resin, copper alloy, glass
Height (overall) 85.6 cm; length (pedestal) 79 cm; width (pedestal) 40 cm
Found in a shrine-shaped box in the Treasury

Travel to the next world was not thought to be simple. Elaborate preparations were required to ensure a safe passage to the kingdom of Osiris, a journey made not only by the dead but also by the sun, which traveled through the netherworld each night. This fierce leopard, painted black to associate it with rebirth, guides and guards Tutankhamun on his journey after death. He wears the tall white crown of Upper Egypt. The flail in one hand and a long staff are also symbols of authority.

The king represented here may not have been intended to be Tutankhamun. There are feminine qualities in this figure, such as the breasts, so this must have been made for Nefertiti after she became king as Ankhkheperure.

May your *ka* live,
and may you pass a million years,
one who loves Thebes and dwells in it,
your face toward the north wind;
may your eyes see the wonderful things.

I would like to thank the many people who have helped me to finish this great book, which celebrates the hundred years that have passed since the discovery of the tomb of Tutankhamun.

First, I would like to thank my assistant, Maryan Ragheb, who witnessed me writing this catalogue every day, helped me with some of the research on the objects of the exhibit, and also sent my handwritten manuscripts to my colleague Noreen Doyle.

Also, thanks to Sophie Ammerman, the young French archaeologist who came for a one-month internship in my office. She read the catalogue for typographical errors.

And I would like to give my thanks to my colleagues Raymond Johnson, Janice Kamrin, and Tarek El Awady. They all gave me invaluable suggestions.

I would like to thank Dr. Khaled El-Enany for sending this exhibit abroad and for creating the best publicity for Egypt, as well as for bringing funds for the restoration of our monuments.

I would like to thank those who went to great efforts to organize this exhibit, which will tour ten cities all around the world: Steven Flint Wood, John Norman, and Andres Numhauser.

And last but not least, I would like to thank my colleague Noreen Doyle, who worked very hard to edit this book in a short time to meet our deadline. I also wish to thank her because she is one of the few people who can read my handwriting from my notes on "yellow pages," and, finally, because she offered great suggestions to me. To Noreen, I give my deepest gratitude for her work.

ABOUT THE AUTHOR

Zahi Hawass is the world's most famous Egyptologist. He has made major discoveries that have captured the hearts of the people all over the world. He discovered the mummies of the family of Tutankhamun and revealed the mystery of his death. He has lectured all over the world and has written twelve books on the life of Tutankhamun. Hawass had been featured in *Time* magazine as one of the top 100 most influential people. In 2017, Hawass received six international prizes, among them: Ambassador of Cultural Heritage for the United Nations, the Golden Column at the film festival in Catanzaro, Italy, and Man of the Year from the Telemed Foundation in Newport Beach-California.

Cover and interior Design by Tooko Mitsui

Printed in China

Credits & Acknowledgments

Produced and published by

 **MELCHER
MEDIA**

124 West 13th Street New York, NY 10011
www.melcher.com

President, CEO: Charles Melcher
VP, COO: Bonnie Eldon
Executive Editor/Producer: Lauren Nathan
Production Director: Susan Lynch
Editor/Producer: Josh Raab
Senior Digital Producer: Shannon Fanuko
Assistant Editor/Producer: Karl Daum

Melcher Media would like to thank Jess Bass, Emma Blackwood,
Renee Bollier, Tova Carlin, Amélie Cherlin, Bart Cooke, Barbara Gogan,
Ashley Gould, Emily Kao, Aaron Kenedi, Samantha Klein, Karolina Manko,
Emma McIntosh, Gabrielle Sirkin, Victoria Spencer, Megan Worman,
Katy Yudin, Gabe Zetter.

IMG

To organize an exhibition of this magnitude, it takes the dedication
and hard work of many talented individuals. I would like to thank our entire
team for doing such an incredible job.

—John Norman–Managing Director IMG Exhibitions

IMG Exhibitions would like to give special thanks to: Dr. Khaled El-Enany,
Dr. Zahi Hawass, Dr. Tarek El Awady, Elham El Mongy, Stephen Flint
Wood, Sam Zussman, Richard Guest-Gornall, Richard Warren, Troy Collins,
Cynthia Brown, Christina Wright, Jason Simmons, Sharon Simpson,
Tom Fricker, Dan Perina, Amanda Wambach, Heather Watson,
David Mauk, Maryan Ragheb, Noreen Doyle, Donna Lawrence Productions,
Brad Malkus, Bryan Harris, Laura Calliari, Kris Easterday, Andres
Numhauser and Design Electronics.

Expert Editorial Consultant: Noreen Doyle, MA
Creative & Editorial Consultant: Cynthia Brown